TREES

This book belongs to:

Atlas Cedar

Where does it grow? Originally from the Atlas Mountains, it was introduced to Britain in the 1840s and prefers dry, sandy, or lime-rich conditions especially in large gardens or parks. ***Height*** Up to 37 metres (120 ft). ***Shape*** Pyramid shaped with upward-pointing branches. ***Leaf*** Dark-green or bluish-green needles. ***Flower*** Pinkish male cones resemble catkins; female cone shaped like a wasps' nest. ***Bark*** Dark grey in fine plates and with deep, narrow cracks. In which continent are the Atlas Mountains?

I-Spy for **15**
Double with answer

Female cone
*I-Spy for **15***

Deodar

Where does it grow? This tree was introduced into Britain from the Himalayas in 1831. It is used as a decorative tree in parks, gardens, and even cemeteries. ***Height*** Up to 65 metres (213 ft) in its natural surroundings but limited to about 34 metres (110 ft) in Britain. ***Shape*** Pyramid shaped with drooping branches. ***Leaf*** Dark-green needles. ***Flower*** Upright dark-purple male cones; rounded, barrel-like female cones. ***Bark*** Greyish brown and cracked into rectangular-shaped plates. *I-Spy for **15***

Incense Cedar

Where does it grow? Coming from North America, this tree was introduced into Britain as an ornamental in 1853. Strictly, this is a member of the Cypress family rather than a cedar. ***Height*** Up to 35 metres (115 ft). ***Shape*** A dense, narrow column like a fountain pen. ***Leaf*** Bright-green, short scales. ***Flower*** Male flowers are yellow while greenish female flowers grow into rich-brown, almost bud-like cones. ***Bark*** Dark red-brown and flaking.

How does this tree get its name?

*I-Spy for **20***
Double with answer

Japanese Red Cedar

Where does it grow? In Japan, as in Britain to which it was introduced in the mid-eighteenth century, it is commonly used as a garden ornamental and shade tree. ***Height*** Up to 50 metres (165 ft) in its native Japan but usually no more than 35 metres (115 feet) in Britain. ***Shape*** A narrow, dense pyramid. ***Leaf*** Short, bright-green needles. ***Flower*** Male flowers form in clusters at the tips of shoots; green female flowers develop into round, dark-brown cones with hooks on the scales. ***Bark*** Light to dark brown peeling away in strips or shreds.

*I-Spy for **15***

Cedar of Lebanon

Where does it grow?
Originally from parts of Turkey, Syria, and, of course, the Lebanon, this tree was introduced to Britain as an ornamental for parks and large gardens more than 300 years ago.
Height Up to 40 metres (130 ft).
Shape Very characteristic with a flat top and branches which level out. **Leaf** Dark-green needles.
Flower Erect cigar-shaped male flowers and green female flowers which grow into upright, barrel-shaped cones. **Bark** Dark greyish brown with short ridges and deep cracks.

I-Spy for **15**

I-Spy cones for **15**

Pencil Cedar

Where does it grow? It was introduced into Britain from North America in the mid-seventeenth century and it prefers drier soils. ***Height*** Up to 30 metres (100 ft) in the wild but usually no more than 15 metres (50 ft) when grown as an ornamental. ***Shape*** A straight stem with a narrowly pyramid-shaped arrangement of upward-growing branches. ***Leaf*** Narrow, bright-green needles at first darkening and shortening to scales. ***Flower*** Male flowers at the leaf tips are yellowish while the female flowers are small and green at first before developing into egg-shaped cones which change from green to brownish violet in colour. ***Bark*** Reddish brown and peels off as strips.
I-Spy for **20**

White Cedar

Where does it grow? Originally from North America, it was one of the first trees to be introduced into Britain some time in the 1500s. It prefers damp soils. **Height** Up to 20 metres (66 ft). Dwarf varieties are grown in small gardens. **Shape** A narrow cone with upward-pointing branches. **Leaf** Dark-green scales which are yellower beneath. **Flower** Small male flowers are reddish brown while the greenish or purple female flowers develop into open, scaly, bud-like cones. **Bark** Orange-brown in colour with vertical cracks.
I-Spy for **15**

Lawson Cypress

Where does it grow?
This tree was introduced into Britain from western North America about 150 years ago. It prefers soils with reasonable amounts of moisture.
Height Up to 50 metres (165 ft).
Shape A narrow cone shape with short branches and hanging foliage. *Leaf* Light-green scales. *Flower* Male flowers are reddish when ripe while the small yellowish female flowers develop into spiky globes. *Bark* Mainly smooth and brown but can develop fine cracks.
I-Spy for **15**

There is also a Gold variety of the Lawson Cypress (right)
I-Spy for **15**

6

Douglas Fir

Where does it grow?
This conifer comes from the west coast of North America and was introduced into Britain in the early 1800s. It grows best on good soils. ***Height*** Up to 100 metres (330 ft) in its native home and up to 55 metres (180 ft) in Britain. ***Shape*** Straight, open branched, and conical. ***Leaf*** Dark-green needles with a groove on the top surface and two white lines beneath. ***Flower*** Yellow male flowers and red tassel-shaped female flowers which develop into down-ward-hanging cones that have three-pointed plates on the scales. ***Bark*** Greyish green on young trees but becoming reddish purple and ridged on older trees.

I-Spy for **15**

Juniper

Where does it grow?
Throughout Britain
and Europe on a
variety of soils
including on
mountainsides.
Height Usually no
more than 15 metres
(50 feet). **Shape**
Usually conical with
upward-pointing
branches but it may
broaden into a
rounder shape with
age. In some areas it
stays as a straggly
shrub. **Leaf** Pointed,
bluish-green needles.
Flower Male and
female flowers grow
on separate trees.
Male flower is small
and yellow while the
female flower is green
and develops into
berries which are
green at first, then
turn purple. **Bark**
Reddish brown and
peeling in strips and
sheets. What are the
berries often used
for?

I-Spy for **15**
Double with answer

*I-Spy berries
for* **15**

European Larch

Where does it grow? It was introduced into Britain from Europe in the seventeenth century. It grows well in dry areas. *Height* In some cases up to 50 metres (165 feet). *Shape* Usually a narrow cone but, in windswept areas, a lower, more straggling shape. *Leaf* Soft, pale-green needles which are lost in winter. *Flower* The male cone-like flowers are yellow while the red female flowers develop into erect, egg-shaped cones. *Bark* Greyish brown and falling away in scale-like plates.

I-Spy tor **15**

I-Spy cones for **15**

9

Japanese Larch

Where does it grow? As its name suggests, it comes from Japan and was introduced to Britain in the 1860s. It grows well in damp conditions. ***Height*** Up to 40 metres (130 ft). ***Shape*** A broad cone with roughly horizontal branches. ***Leaf*** Bluish-green needles with white bands beneath. They fall in winter. ***Flower*** Yellow, globe-shaped male flowers and greenish, egg-shaped female flowers which develop into rounded cones with scales that turn outwards. ***Bark*** Reddish brown and scaly.

I-Spy for **20**

Maidenhair Tree (Ginkgo)

Where does it grow? This ancient tree has been grown in Japan and China for hundreds of years and was introduced to Britain in the eighteenth century. It tolerates most conditions. ***Height*** Up to 30 metres (100 feet). ***Shape*** A narrow cone shape at first becoming massive and straggly. ***Leaf*** Fan shaped and sometimes divided in the middle. ***Flower*** Male flowers resemble catkins while the small round female flowers, which grow on separate trees, develop into green, egg-shaped fruits. ***Bark*** Brown, rough, and corky.

I-Spy for **25**

I-Spy leaves for **15**

Monkey Puzzle Tree

Where does it grow?
Originally from Chile and Argentina, it was introduced into Britain in the eighteenth century by a Cornish man who said 'It would puzzle a monkey to climb the tree'. *Height* Up to 30 metres (100 ft). *Shape* Cone shaped or rather domed with

irregular branches. *Leaf* Triangular and dark green, overlapping, and completely covering the branches. *Flower* Male cones occur in clusters, while the female cones are globe shaped.
Bark Dark grey and marked with rings.
I-Spy for 15

Corsican Pine (Austrian Pine)

Where does it grow? Originating in central and southern Europe, it was introduced into Britain in 1835 where it will tolerate poor, dry, chalky soils. *Height* Up to 40 metres (130 ft). *Shape* Roughly pyramid shaped but becoming more flat topped as the tree ages. *Leaf* Long, stiff needles arranged like the head of a besom. *Flower* Clusters of yellow male

flowers and pairs of female flowers which grow into large, brown, egg-shaped cones. *Bark* Rough and dark greyish brown.
I-Spy for 20

Scots Pine
Where does it grow?
Throughout Europe and parts of Asia on light mountain soils. In Britain, it is native only to Scotland.
Height Up to 35 metres (115 feet).
Shape The young tree is a typical pyramid-shaped conifer but, as the tree ages, it loses its lower branches and the top flattens. *Leaf* Longish paired needles which usually twist. *Flower* Yellow male flowers and red female flowers which grow into egg-shaped cones that release winged seeds. *Bark* Red and cracking.
I-Spy for **10**

I-Spy leaves for **10**

I-Spy cones for **10**

Coast Redwood

Where does it grow? Originally from the Pacific coast of North America, it was introduced into Britain in the mid-1800s as an ornamental for large parks and gardens. ***Height*** The world's tallest tree, it can reach 120 metres (400 ft) in the wild. ***Shape*** Column shaped with a thick trunk. ***Leaf*** Flattened needles which go brown in winter. ***Flower*** Male flowers are yellow; female flowers are green and develop into rounded cones. ***Bark*** Reddish, soft, and seeming to be made up of fibres. It protects the tree from fire. How long can a Coast Redwood live?

*I-Spy for **20** – double with answer*

Norway Spruce

Where does it grow? This tree once grew as a native in Britain but was reintroduced from northern Europe almost 500 years ago. It is the typical 'Christmas tree'. ***Height*** Up to 60 metres (200 ft) in the wild state. ***Shape*** Cone shaped with top branches upward pointing and lower branches more drooping. ***Leaf*** Short, prickly, pale-green needles. ***Flower*** Male flowers are yellow; female flowers are pinkish and develop into long, cylindrical cones. ***Bark*** Smooth, pale reddish brown.
*I-Spy for **10***

Sitka Spruce

Where does it grow? The Sitka Spruce was introduced into Britain from North America in the 1830s. It prefers damp soils. ***Height*** Up to 50 metres (165 ft). ***Shape*** Cone shaped with long lower branches and a thick trunk. ***Leaf*** Long, thin, prickly, dark bluish-green needles. ***Flower*** Yellow male flowers like catkins and reddish female flowers which develop into cigar-shaped cones. ***Bark*** Greyish brown and peeling off in plates.

I-Spy for **15**

Wellingtonia (Giant Redwood)

Where does it grow? Originally from the slopes of the Sierra Nevada mountains on the west coast of North America, it was introduced into Britain in the mid-1800s to be used in large parks and gardens, and avenues as an ornamental. ***Height*** Up to 90 metres (295 ft) in the wild. The trunk can measure 7 metres (23 ft) round. ***Shape*** Narrowly conical. ***Leaf*** Scale-like and changing from green to brown in colour. ***Flower*** Male flowers are yellow; the green female flowers develop into egg-shaped cones. ***Bark*** Ribbed, reddish brown to near black, fibre-like. The world's most massive tree is found in the Sequoia National Park in America. What is the tree called?

I-Spy for **20** *– double with answer*

Yew

Where does it grow?
Throughout Europe, especially on chalky soils. **Height** Up to 20 metres (65 ft). **Shape** A broad, rounded cone sometimes with a many divided trunk. **Leaf** Flattened needles dark green above and paler beneath. **Flower** The male flowers are small yellow globes; female flowers are tiny and greenish and develop into red berries. **Bark** Reddish brown, flaking and peeling. Note: the bark, foliage, and seeds are poisonous. For what purpose was Yew wood valued in the Middle Ages?

*I-Spy for **10***
Double with answer

*I-Spy fruit for **10***

Common Alder
Where does it grow?
From Britain through Europe to Asia where it will grow in water-logged soils so it is often seen by rivers and ponds. ***Height*** Up to 20 metres (65 ft). ***Shape*** Cone shaped with regularly arranged branches. ***Leaf*** Almost round with wavy or toothed edges. ***Flower*** Long male catkins and small, more globe-shaped female catkins on the same tree. ***Fruit*** A small nut with a narrow wing; it will float on water. ***Bark*** Rough, greyish brown, and platy.
I-Spy for **10**

Apple

Where does it grow? The edible Apple is usually cultivated in orchards or gardens. **Height** Up to 15 metres (50 ft) but nowadays, smaller trees, or trained or grafted trees are usually grown. **Shape** Variable. **Leaf** Oval with a rounded base and serrated edges. **Flower** White or pinkish, five-petalled flowers usually in clusters. **Fruit** Apple. Throughout Europe, at least 1000 different kinds of Apple have been developed although, now, relatively few varieties are grown widely. **Bark** Greyish brown and may flake when old.

I-Spy for **5**

Crab Apple

Where does it grow? Throughout much of Britain and Europe, especially in oak woods. It is the ancestor of the cultivated Apple. **Height** Up to 10 metres (33 ft). **Shape** Rounded and shrub-like. **Leaf** Oval with a pointed tip and serrated edges. **Flower** Usually white, five petalled, and in clusters. **Fruit** Small, bitter-tasting, yellowish-green, or red apples. The fruit may be used for making jellies and jams. **Bark** Greyish brown and may flake when old. Some trees may be thorny.

I-Spy for **10**

I-Spy blossom for **10**

Ash

Where does it grow?
Throughout Britain and Europe, especially on damp soils.
Height Up to 40 metres (130 ft).
Shape A tall dome with irregular branches. **Leaf** The leaflets are spear shaped and pointed with toothed edges. They make an opposite arrangement on the stem. **Flower** Both male and female flowers appear on the same tree and are purplish in colour.
Fruit Single-winged seeds in clusters.
Bark Pale greenish grey, and becoming ridged and cracked in old trees.

I-Spy for **10**

Aspen
Where does it grow?
Throughout Britain and Europe, especially on damp soils in hills and valleys.
Height Up to 20 metres (65 ft). **Shape** Open and roughly conical crown with upward-pointing branches. **Leaf** Spade shaped with a pointed tip and wavy edges. The slightest breeze makes the leaves tremble. **Flower** Male and female catkins are long and grow on separate trees. Male catkins are brown, females green. **Fruit** Woolly seeds. **Bark** Greyish green with a diamond-shaped pattern of grooves.
I-Spy for **15**

I-Spy leaves for **15**

Beech

Where does it grow?
Throughout Britain
and Europe, espe-
cially on chalk. *Height*
Up to 40 metres (130
ft). *Shape* A massive,
spreading dome-
shaped crown. *Leaf*
Oval with a pointed tip
and wavy margins.
Bright green and
waxy. A common
ornamental variety,
called a Copper
Beech, has reddish-
purple leaves. *Flower*
Male flowers occur in
clusters and female
flowers in pairs on the
same tree. *Fruit*
Triangular nuts held in
pairs in a rough husk.
Bark Smooth and
grey. Beech wood is
traditionally used to
make chairs. What is
the chairmaker
called?

I-Spy for **5**
Double with answer

I-Spy Copper
Beech for **15**

Downy Birch

Where does it grow? It usually grows best on poor, damp, and peaty soils throughout much of Britain and Europe. *Height* Up to 25 metres (82 feet). *Shape* It has a rounded, oval crown with quite thick and open-looking branches. *Leaf* Oval with serrated edges and hairy veins on the underside. *Flower* Female catkin is small, upright and yellowish while the larger male catkin turns from green to brownish and hangs down. *Fruit* A winged nutlet. *Bark* Usually reddish brown but may be grey.

I-Spy for **15**

I-Spy catkins for **15**

Silver Birch

Where does it grow? Throughout much of Britain and Europe on most soils. It is hardy and often the first tree to grow on an area of land. *Height* Up to 30 metres (100 ft) but usually less. *Shape* Similar to the Downy Birch but with closer-growing and more drooping branches. *Leaf* Spade shaped with a straight base and serrated edges. *Flower* Upright green female catkin and yellowish, hanging male catkin. *Fruit* A winged nutlet. *Bark* As the tree ages, it becomes the well-known silver colour marked with black.

I-Spy for **5**

Blackthorn

Where does it grow? Hedgerows and thickets throughout much of Britain and Europe. *Height* Up to 6 metres (20 ft). *Shape* A branched and bushy small tree or shrub with thorns. *Leaf* Oval with a pointed tip and toothed edges. *Flower* Five-petalled white flowers blossom before the leaves appear. *Fruit* A dark-blue berry, called a Sloe, about the size of a large pea. The berry often has a greyish bloom. *Bark* Blackish brown. What is the name of the Irish cudgel traditionally made from a Blackthorn branch?

I-Spy for 10 – double with answer

I-Spy Sloe for 15

Common Buckthorn

Where does it grow? In hedges, thickets, and woodland edges on chalky soils throughout much of Britain and Europe. *Height* Up to 9 metres (30 ft). *Shape* A small, dense, shrub-like, thorny tree. *Leaf* Bright green, oval, and toothed. *Flower* Four petalled and greenish yellow with male and female flowers on separate trees. *Fruit* Small clusters of round, black berries. *Bark* Dark brown or almost black, scaly, and cracked to show orange.
I-Spy for 15

I-Spy in autumn colours for 15

Bird Cherry

Where does it grow? Throughout much of Britain and Europe, especially on lime-rich soils. ***Height*** Up to 16 metres (52 ft). ***Shape*** A roughly oval-shaped crown with upward-pointing branches. ***Leaf*** A long oval shape with pointed tip and finely toothed edges. ***Flower*** The whole tree may be swathed in spikes of five-petalled, almond-scented, white flowers. ***Fruit*** A small blackish cherry with a very bitter taste. ***Bark*** Dark greyish brown and smooth.
I-Spy for **15**

Wild Cherry (Gean)

Where does it grow? Throughout much of Britain and Europe especially on clay over a chalk bedrock. ***Height*** Up to 25 metres (82 ft). ***Shape*** The crown is roughly a pyramid shape. ***Leaf*** Spear shaped and pointed with toothed edges. ***Flower*** Clusters of five-petalled, white flowers. ***Fruit*** Bright-red cherries which may be sweet or sour. ***Bark*** Reddish brown and peeling in strips.
I-Spy for **15**

Horse Chestnut
Where does it grow?
Originally from mountain woodlands in the Balkans, it was introduced into Britain in the 1500s. ***Height*** Up to 35 metres (115 ft). ***Shape*** A massive, spreading, dome-shaped crown on a thick trunk. ***Leaf*** Each leaf is made up of five to seven spear-shaped leaflets with tapering bases, rather like a spread hand. ***Flower*** A pyramid-shaped spike of white or sometimes pinkish-red flowers. ***Fruit*** The

well-known, shiny brown 'conker' contained in a spiny shell. ***Bark*** Dark greyish or reddish brown. Where does the name 'conker' come from?

I-Spy for **5** – double with answer

I-Spy flower buds opening for **10**

I-Spy Red Horse Chestnut for **15**

Sweet Chestnut
Where does it grow?
Originally from the area around the Mediterranean, most Sweet Chestnuts in Britain have been planted. This tree prefers a well-drained soil. **Height** Up to 30 metres (100 ft).
Shape Tall and column shaped when young but the lower branches become more spreading with age. **Leaf** Spear shaped and saw toothed with parallel veins. **Flower** The male flowers are long, yellow catkins while the female flowers are small and greenish.
Fruit The well-known chestnut contained in groups of two or three in a spiny green husk.
Bark Brownish grey with spiral-shaped grooves running upwards.
I-Spy for **15**

I-Spy autumn leaves for **15**

Elder

Where does it grow? Throughout much of Europe, especially in damp woods and hedgerows. **Height** Up to 10 metres (33 ft) but often just a many stemmed shrub. **Shape** The tree has a domed crown. **Leaf** Five to seven toothed leaflets are arranged oppositely on a stem. **Flower** Sprays of small, white-petalled flowers which are pleasantly scented at first and then tend to smell of tomcats. **Fruit** Clusters of small reddish-black berries. **Bark** Light greyish brown. Elders often grow near to badger setts. True or False?

I-Spy for 5 – double with answer

English Elm

Where does it grow?
Throughout Europe, especially in hedgerows. Most trees in Britain were planted from nursery-grown seedlings and were very prone to so-called Dutch elm disease. At least 80 per cent of the trees died. **Height** Up to 40 metres (130 ft).
Shape Tall, elegant, and with a narrowly domed crown. **Leaf** A rounded oval with a bluntly pointed tip and serrated edges.
Flower Dense clusters with prominent red anthers.
Fruit A winged seed.
Bark Dark brown with deep vertical cracks.
I-Spy for **15**

I-Spy fruits for **25**

27

Smooth-leaved Elm
Where does it grow?
Throughout much of Europe but in Britain it is found only in the warmer areas of the south and east. **Height** Up to 30 metres (100 ft). **Shape** Narrowly domed with branches that point upwards at first and then droop at the tips. **Leaf** Bright green, oval, and with a pointed tip and toothed edges. The top is smooth and shiny. **Flower** Similar to that of English Elm but red. **Fruit** A winged seed. **Bark** Dark brown and deeply cracked.
I-Spy for **15**

Wych Elm
Where does it grow?
Throughout Britain and Europe in most conditions. **Height** Up to 40 metres (130 ft). **Shape** The crown is a broad, spreading dome. **Leaf** Oval, toothed, and with a pointed tip. **Flower** Similar to that of English Elm but looking rather purplish. **Fruit** A winged seed. **Bark** Greyish brown with long cracks. How does this tree get its name?

I-Spy for **15** – double with answer

Handkerchief Tree

Where does it grow? Originally from China, it was introduced into Britain about 100 years ago as an ornamental for parks and gardens. ***Height*** Up to 20 metres (66 ft) in the wild but usually less in cultivation. ***Shape*** This is a slender tree with a broadly conical crown. ***Leaf*** Large, heart shaped, with a pointed tip and with serrated edges. ***Flower*** This is purple but is partly enclosed by two, white, leaf-like flaps which give the tree its name. ***Fruit*** A large fruit which turns from green to purple. ***Bark*** Greyish brown and finely cracked.

I-Spy for **25**

Hawthorn

Where does it grow? Throughout Britain and Europe especially on lime-rich soils. ***Height*** Up to 15 metres (50 ft). ***Shape*** Variable but in single trees it may have a globe-shaped crown. ***Leaf*** Generally a long oval in shape and consisting of three to five lobes with a few teeth at the tips. ***Flower*** Clusters of five-petalled, usually white (but sometimes pink) blossoms. ***Fruit*** Small, round berries which are green at first but bright red when ripe. ***Bark*** Greyish brown and scaly. What other names do you know for this tree?

I-Spy for **5** *– double with answer*

Hazel

Where does it grow?
Throughout Britain and most of Europe. **Height** Up to 12 metres (40 ft). **Shape** Usually the trunk is short and the crown oval shaped and bushy with upward-growing branches. **Leaf** Heart shaped with toothed edges. **Flower** Tiny red female flowers and the familiar long yellow catkins or 'lambs' tails'. **Fruit** One to four nuts in clusters. **Bark** Pale brown and rather scaly. What is coppicing?

I-Spy for **5** double with answer	
I-Spy fruits for **10**	
I-Spy catkins for **10**	

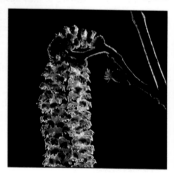

Holly

Where does it grow? Throughout much of Britain and Europe on most kinds of soil provided it is not waterlogged. ***Height*** Sometimes up to 25 metres (82 ft) but more often half that height. ***Shape*** A rounded cone shape. ***Leaf*** Generally spear shaped, wavy, and prickly. Dark green and waxy. This is an evergreen tree. ***Flower*** Clusters of small, pinkish-white, sweet-scented flowers. ***Fruit*** Blood-red berries on female-flowered trees only. ***Bark*** Silvery grey and smooth.

I-Spy for 5 I-Spy berries for **15**

Hornbeam

Where does it grow? Native to most of Europe including south-east England. ***Height*** Up to 25 metres (82 ft). ***Shape*** Generally globe-shaped crown on short-fluted trunk with upward-pointing branches. ***Leaf*** Broadly

spear shaped with a pointed tip and serrated edges. The veins on the underside are hairy. ***Flower*** Yellow male catkins and small female flowers with red styles. ***Fruit*** Clusters of nuts, each surrounded by a three-lobed, leaf-like structure. ***Bark*** Smooth and dark grey.

I-Spy for 10

Large-leaved Lime

Where does it grow?
Native to southern and central Europe, it is commonly planted as avenues and in parks and large public gardens. *Height* Up to 35 metres (115 ft) *Shape* Column shaped with upward-pointing branches. *Leaf* Large, heart shaped, and hairy. (The leaves of the similar Small-leaved

Lime may be less than half the size.) *Flower* Sweet-scented, five-petalled, greenish-yellow flowers. *Fruit* Small clusters of globe-shaped fruits. *Bark* Dark grey and quite smooth but with fine cracks.

I-Spy for **5** ☐   I-Spy leaves for **5** ☐   I-Spy fruits for **10** ☐

Locust Tree

Where does it grow? Originally from North America, it was introduced into Europe in the seventeenth century and then into Britain where it grows on light soils in the south of England. *Height* Up to 25 metres (82 ft). *Shape* It has a broad, open crown and twisting branches. *Leaf* Alternate oval leaflets with short spines at the tips, in pairs along the leaf stem. *Flower* Hanging clusters of white, scented, pea-like blossoms. *Fruit* Clusters of brown pods containing black, kidney-shaped seeds. *Bark* Greyish brown with twisting ridges and grooves.

I-Spy for **25** ☐

Magnolia

Where does it grow?
Originally from
America, it was
introduced into Europe
in the late eighteenth
century. **Height** Up to
30 metres (100 ft) in
the wild but usually
smaller in cultivation.
Shape Tall, oval, and
rather unruly. **Leaf**
Spear shaped with a
pointed tip and softly

hairy beneath. **Flower** Large white flowers tinted with pink or reddish
purple. **Fruit** Similar to a cone. **Bark** Smooth and dull greyish.
I-Spy for 20

Field Maple

Where does it grow? In Britain, mainly on chalk soils in the south.
Height Up to 26 metres (85 ft) **Shape** A globe-shaped crown with
branches that turn up at the tips. **Leaf** Roughly triangular but consisting
of three large lobes and two
smaller ones at the base. **Flower**
Upright clusters of small yellowish-
green flowers. **Fruit** Clusters of
four paired winged seeds. **Bark**
Greyish brown with fine, almost
orange-coloured cracks. What is
the type of Maple wood used by
furniture makers called?

I-Spy for **15** – double with answer

Japanese Maple

Where does it grow?
Native to Japan,
varieties of this tree
are common in British
parks and gardens.
Height Up to 15
metres (50 ft). ***Shape***
Spreading and bushy
with a short, twisting
trunk. ***Leaf*** Each long-
stemmed leaf consists
of five or seven,
spear-shaped pointed
lobes with serrated
edges. ***Flower*** Clusters of small, dark purplish-red flowers. ***Fruit*** Clusters
of paired winged seeds. ***Bark*** Greyish brown in older trees.
I-Spy for **20**

Paperbark Maple

Where does it grow? Originally
from China, it was introduced into
Britain as recently as 1901, but it is
now a very popular ornamental
tree. ***Height*** Up to 14 metres (46
ft). ***Shape*** An open, upright, rather
dome-shaped crown. ***Leaf*** Each
leaf is made up of three lobed
leaflets. ***Flower*** Clusters of small,
yellow, hanging flowers. ***Fruit***
Clusters of
winged seeds
in horseshoe-
shaped pairs.
Bark Rich
reddish brown
and peels off in
papery strips.
I-Spy for **20**

Medlar

Where does it grow? Originally from south-eastern Europe, it has been cultivated in southern England for centuries and some trees are now effectively wild. ***Height*** Up to 6 metres (20 ft). ***Shape*** A spreading, straggling tree on a short trunk. ***Leaf*** Narrowly spear shaped with fine teeth near the tip. ***Flower*** Single, five-petalled white flowers at the tip of each twig. ***Fruit*** When ripe, it is a yellowish-brown globe surrounded by the petals. It is edible only after it has been frosted. ***Bark*** Greyish brown and cracked into rectangular plates.

I-Spy for **25**

Black Mulberry

Where does it grow? Possibly it came originally from the Middle or Far East, but it has been cultivated for so long, no one is sure. The Romans probably introduced it to Britain. ***Height*** Up to 10 metres (33 ft) but usually less. ***Shape*** The crown is thick and spreading with twisting branches. ***Leaf*** Heart shaped, saw toothed, with a pointed tip, and hairy on both sides. ***Flowers*** Cylindrical, catkin-like flowers with the females about half the length of the males. ***Fruit*** Deep-purple, raspberry-like fruits which are sour until they are well ripened. ***Bark*** Rough, scaly, and orange-brown in colour. What rhyme includes this tree?

I-Spy for **20** *– double with answer*

Common Oak (English Oak)

Where does it grow? Throughout most of Europe as single trees or forming woodlands with other deciduous trees. *Height* Up to 45 metres (150 ft). *Shape* A strong-looking, spreading, domed tree with thick, twisting branches. *Leaf* Roughly oblong in shape but the edges are divided into between five and seven rounded lobes. *Flowers* Small female flowers and clusters of long, open male catkins. *Fruit* The well-known acorns set in scaly cups grouped at the end of a stem. *Bark* Brownish grey and cracked into vertical plates.

I-Spy for 5

I-Spy acorns for 10

Holm Oak

Where does it grow?
Originally from the lands around the Mediterranean, it was introduced into Britain as an ornamental and shade tree in the sixteenth century. **Height** Up to 25 metres (82 ft). **Shape** A broad, round dome. **Leaf** Roughly spear shaped with spiny edges when young and becoming narrower and smoother with age — quite unlike a 'typical' oak leaf. **Flowers** Similar to other oaks. **Fruit** Green acorns, almost enclosed by the scaly cup. **Bark** Dark greyish brown, and seeming to be made up of small plates.

I-Spy for **10**

I-Spy acorns for **15**

Sessile Oak

Where does it grow? In woods on light, sandy soils throughout Britain and Europe. **Height** Up to 40 metres (130 ft). **Shape** A roughly globe-shaped crown with branches pointing upwards from a trunk which is less thick than a Common Oak's. **Leaf** Similar to that of the Common Oak but on a stem. **Flowers** Typical of all oaks. **Fruit** The acorns have no stalks or only very short ones — hence the name 'Sessile'. **Bark** Greyish and finely cracked into plates like that of the Common Oak.

I-Spy for **5**

Turkey Oak

Where does it grow? From south-eastern and south-central Europe as its name suggests. It was introduced into Britain more than 100 years ago. It thrives on lime-rich soils. **Height** Up to 38 metres (125 ft) in the wild. **Shape** Dome shaped and with a straight trunk. **Leaf** Longer and narrower than 'typical' oaks and with more frequent and pointed lobes. **Flowers** Similar to other oaks. **Fruit** The acorns are held in softly bristly cups. **Bark** Greyish and deeply cracked to make it rougher than the British oaks.

I-Spy for **10**

I-Spy acorns for **15**

Pear

Where does it grow? Originally
from western Asia, Pears have
been cultivated in different
varieties for their fruit for thou-
sands of years. They do not grow
well in very cold or dry conditions.
Height Up to 20 metres (65 ft) in
the wild but cultivated trees are not
so tall. *Shape* Narrow, open, and
often leaning. Sometimes thorny.
Leaf Oval with toothed margins
and a bluntly pointed tip. Dark
green. *Flower* Clusters of white,
five-petalled flowers. *Fruit* The fruit
of the wild trees is small, sour, and
has a gritty texture. *Bark* Dark
reddish or greyish brown
and cracked into plates.
I-Spy for 10

London Plane

Where does it grow? This tree is a cross between the American Plane
and the Oriental Plane and may have been grown in Britain more than
300 years ago. It is tolerant of air pollution so that it survives in the busy
London squares and streets. *Height* Up to 35 metres (115 ft). *Shape*
Dense and dome shaped with twisting braches. *Leaf* Usually three or
five main lobes with
further pointed smaller
lobes. *Flower* Both
sexes are roughly
spherical but female
flowers are larger and
reddish while the males
are yellow. *Fruit* A
rather bur-like fruit
contains the seeds.
Bark Dark greyish
brown, peeling in flakes
to show yellowy
orange beneath.
I-Spy for 10

Black Poplar

Where does it grow? Throughout much of Britain and Europe especially along roadsides. The Lombardy Poplar, introduced into Britain from

Italy, is a variety of this tree and has a characteristic, tall, column shape with steeply upward-pointing branches. ***Height*** Up to 30 metres (100 ft). ***Shape*** A medium-sized, spreading tree on a short trunk. ***Leaf*** Almost heart shaped but with a pointed tip and base. They turn yellow in autumn. ***Flower*** Red male catkins and greenish female catkins which become fluffy when they are about to drop the seeds. ***Fruit*** Fluffy seeds. ***Bark*** Greyish brown with knobs and cracks.

I-Spy for **10**

I-Spy Lombardy Poplar for **10**

White Poplar

Where does it grow? Throughout Europe, especially on damp soils, and was probably introduced into Britain about 400 years ago. ***Height*** Up to 20 metres (66 ft). ***Shape*** A broad, roughly dome-shaped crown which may grow more strongly on one side. ***Leaf*** Roughly triangular and lobed like that of a Maple. ***Flower*** Fluffy greenish-white male catkin with tiny red flowers while the female catkin is greenish yellow. ***Fruit*** Fluffy, hanging from the catkins. ***Bark*** Smooth and greyish green or white with rough dark marks in older trees.

*I-Spy for **15***

Rowan (Mountain Ash)

Where does it grow? Throughout most of Europe in many areas, including mountainsides. It is also planted as an ornamental. ***Height*** Up to 20 metres (65 ft). ***Shape*** Open and roughly conical although it may be irregular in windswept areas. ***Leaf*** Each leaf is made up of pairs of opposite, elongated, spear-shaped leaves which are toothed at first. ***Flower*** Clusters of whitish flowers. ***Fruit*** Clusters of bright-red berries. ***Bark*** Smooth and silvery grey.

*I-Spy for **10***

*I-Spy flowers for **15***

*I-Spy berries for **15***

Wild Service Tree

Where does it grow? Found throughout most of Europe but it is now rare in Britain and found mainly in old oak woodland. ***Height*** Up to 20 metres (66 ft). ***Shape*** A spreading conical or domed shape. ***Leaf*** Narrowly triangular, lobed, and toothed. ***Flower*** Clusters of five-petalled white blossoms. ***Fruit*** A round, brown fruit containing brown seeds. ***Bark*** Dark greyish brown with fine cracks.

I-Spy for **10**

Spindle

Where does it grow? Found in many parts of Europe in hedgerows on chalky or lime-rich soils. ***Height*** Up to 6 metres (20 ft). ***Shape*** An open, many branched, shrub-like small tree. ***Leaf*** Narrowly spear shaped, pointed, and toothed. ***Flower*** Loose clusters of four-petalled, yellowish flowers. ***Fruit*** Red, four-lobed capsules containing the seeds. ***Bark***

Smooth and greyish green in young trees becoming rougher and tinged with red. How does it get its name?

I-Spy for **10** *– double with answer*

I-Spy berries for **15**

Stag's-horn Sumac

Where does it grow? Originally probably from North America, it was introduced into Britain as a garden ornamental. *Height* Up to 8 metres (26 ft). *Shape* It gets its name because, in winter, the bare branches look like a deer's antlers. *Leaf* The leaf comprises fronds of paired, opposite, narrowly spear-shaped and toothed leaflets. *Flower* Male flowers are spikes of tiny yellowish flowers while those of the female are reddish. *Fruit* Spiked clusters of globe-shaped fruits. *Bark* Smooth and dark brown.

I-Spy for **25**

Sycamore

Where does it grow? Originally from central and southern Europe, it was introduced into Britain for timber, shade, and as a windbreak. It will grow almost anywhere. *Height* Up to 35 metres (115 ft). *Shape* A domed, spreading, dense crown. *Leaf* Almost square in shape but with three to seven toothed lobes. *Flower* Open, loose, hanging spikes of greenish-yellow blossoms. *Fruit* Clusters of paired, winged seeds. *Bark* Grey and mainly smooth.

I-Spy for **5**

I-Spy seeds for **10**

43

Tulip Tree

Where does it grow?
Originally from North America, this member of the Magnolia family was introduced to Britain in the 1600s. It prefers deep soil.
Height Up to 50 metres (165 ft) in the wild. *Shape* Column shaped when young but becoming a more domed crown with age. *Leaf* Almost square but with four lobes and a rounded base on a long stalk. *Flower* A yellowish-white tulip-like flower. *Fruit* Brown and looking like a bud but made up of winged seeds. *Bark* Greyish brown and smooth at first but becoming ridged.
I-Spy for *20*

I-Spy autumn leaves for *20*

Wayfaring Tree

Where does it grow? Throughout Europe, especially in hedges and thickets on chalky soils. ***Height*** Up to 6 metres (20 ft). ***Shape*** Small, spreading, and shrub-like. ***Leaf*** Oval, toothed, and hairy. ***Flower*** Dense clusters of tiny white blossoms. ***Fruit*** Clusters of slightly flattened berries which are red at first and then turn black.
Bark Greyish brown and hairy.

I-Spy for **10** ☐   *I-Spy flowers for* **10** ☐   *I-Spy fruits for* **10** ☐

Whitebeam

Where does it grow? Throughout Europe, especially on chalky soils but it is also planted in parks and gardens. ***Height*** Up to 25 metres (82 ft). ***Shape*** Roughly domed but can be somewhat spreading. ***Leaf*** Oval, pointed, and toothed, hairy beneath. ***Flower*** Clusters of perfumed white flowers. ***Fruit*** Berries which ripen to bright red. ***Bark*** Smooth, pale greyish brown.
I-Spy for **10** ☐

Crack Willow

Where does it grow? Throughout much of Britain and Europe in damp soils especially by streams and ponds. *Height* Up to 25 metres (82 ft). *Shape* Naturally, it produces a rounded domed crown on a short trunk. *Leaf* Narrowly spear shaped with greyish-green underside. *Flower* Green female catkins and yellow male catkins on separate trees. *Fruit* White, fluffy seeds. *Bark* Dark greyish with deep cracks and ridges. This tree is often pollarded. What is pollarding?

I-Spy for 5
Double with answer

46

Goat Willow (Pussy Willow, Sallow)

Where does it grow? Woods and hedgerows throughout most of Britain and Europe. *Height* Up to 10 metres (33 ft). *Shape* Shrubby and with many branches. *Leaf* Oval, slightly toothed, and hairy on the underside. *Flower* Male and female catkins grow on separate trees. The male catkin is yellowish, the female greenish. *Fruit* The seeds are woolly. *Bark* Pale greyish brown with slight cracking.

I-Spy for **5**

Weeping Willow

Where does it grow? The tree most commonly seen is probably a cross between a Chinese type and a White Willow.. It often grows beside water in parks and gardens. *Height* Up to 20 metres (65 ft). *Shape* A globe-shaped crown of drooping branches which may touch the ground. *Leaf* As willows. *Flower* Typical willow catkins. *Fruit* Woolly seeds. *Bark* Ridged and greyish brown.

I-Spy for **10**

47

INDEX

Answers

Atlas Cedar: Africa.
Incense Cedar: The wood, resin, and leaves are scented.
Juniper: Flavouring gin.
Coast Redwood: 1000 years.
Wellingtonia: The General Sherman Tree.
Yew: For making longbows.
Beech: Bodger.
Blackthorn: Shillelagh.
Horse Chestnut: Conqueror.
Wych Elm: 'Wych' is a Saxon word for bendy.
Hawthorn: May, Quickthorn.
Hazel: Cutting back the tree to produce many long straight poles for such tasks as making wattle hurdles.
Field Maple: Bird's-eye Maple
Black Mulberry: Here we go round the Mulberry Bush.
Spindle: The wood was used for making spinners' spindles.
Crack Willow: The tree is cut back to the trunk to produce lots of long branches for use in making wattle hurdles and the like. Cattle can be allowed to graze where there are pollarded trees because the young shoots are too high for them to eat.

ISBN 1 85671 192 7

Michelin Tyre Public Limited Company
Edward Hyde Building, 38 Clarendon Road, Watford, Herts WD1 1SX

MICHELIN and the Michelin Man are Registered Trademarks of Michelin

A CIP record for this title is available from the British Library.

Edited by Neil Curtis. Designed by Richard Garratt.

The Publisher gratefully acknowledges the contribution of Oxford Scientific Films who provided the majority of the photographs in this I-Spy book. Additional photographs by RIDA Photo Library and Richard Garratt. Cover photographs: Bruce Coleman Limited.

Colour reproduction by Anglia Colour.

Printed in Spain by Graficromo SA.